CONTENTS

THE NEED FOR SHELTER

Most people, if asked to list those things that are really essential in life, would probably place food and shelter at the very top of their list. From the very earliest times, when people lived in caves, down to the present day, people have always looked for shelter to protect themselves from the cold and rain. Sometimes, these were very simple shelters, and sometimes great castles or mansions with many rooms.

In this book we shall look at some of these houses, although, of course, it is impossible to study **every** different type of house.

LOOKING AT YOUR OWN HOUSE

Before looking at houses in the past, let us look at the way houses are built today. Have you ever thought about your own house? Although houses today are built in many different shapes and sizes, most have certain things in common. For example, almost all have walls made of bricks or concrete blocks, glass windows and doors made of wood or aluminium. There are other things about houses today, however, which are not quite so obvious. Most houses have two brick or concrete walls separated by a narrow gap to keep out the rain; and they almost always have drains to carry away the rain water and sewerage. Because these things are not easily seen most people do not think about them very often. They can, however, make a tremendous difference to the way people live.

Houses and Homes
in Wales

Richard Carter and Walter Jones

Welsh Office
History Resources Scheme

GOMER

First Impression—November 1996

ISBN 1 85902 452 1

This resource is published with the financial support of the
Secretary of State for Wales.

Acknowledgements
Line illustrations and diagrams by David Chamberlain.
The authors and publishers would like to thank the following institutions for
permission to reproduce photographic material from their collections:
National Museum of Wales: pages 42, 43 and 47;
Crown copyright: Royal Commission on the Ancient and Historical Monuments
in Wales: pages 22, 31 and back cover.

*Printed at Gomer Press,
Llandysul, Ceredigion*

- Can you think of anything else about the way houses are built today which helps to make them more comfortable for people to live in?

There are also other things about the inside of your house which people often take for granted. For example, houses today are always divided up into separate rooms, often with a separate living room, a kitchen, bathroom and, in many houses, two or more bedrooms. Each of these rooms is used for a different purpose.

- Draw a plan showing the rooms the house, flat or bungalow where you live. You might then try to work out the proportions of the time you and the other members of your family spend in each part of the building.

Now you have thought about houses today, we will look at some of the different types of houses built over the centuries, beginning with those built by the Celts around two thousand years ago and ending with houses built less than a hundred years ago.

Remember too, that when new houses were built, this did not mean that other types of houses suddenly disappeared. In fact, houses built hundreds of years ago are still often found alongside those built in the last few years.

- You might like to make a list of the different kinds of houses around where you live. You might also be able to find out when these houses were first built.

THE HOUSES AND HOMES OF THE CELTS

Historical background

The Celts first arrived in what is now England from Europe around the year 500 BC and began to settle in Wales about a hundred years later. These Celts, divided up into many small tribes, were a very warlike people who were always fighting each other to gain more land. Because they feared attack from their neighbours, most Celts lived in forts built on the hills and surrounded by a strong wooden fence for protection. Eventually, however, as a few powerful tribes, like the Silures in south-east Wales, began to conquer the weaker tribes, the dangers of attack gradually became less. In those areas, although the villages were still surrounded by fences to keep out wild animals, they felt safe enough to plant crops and graze their cattle on land outside the village.

Finding out about the Celts and their homes

Before looking more closely at the homes of the Celts, it is important to remember that it is not always possible to be sure what their villages and houses actually looked like. Here are some of the problems archaeologists, who try to find out what things were like in the distant past, face in trying to build up an accurate picture of the Celts:

    *   Because the Celts built most of their houses of wood which rotted away centuries ago, none of their houses remain standing today.

*   The Celts left no written records or drawings to tell us what their houses looked like.

*   After the Celts had lived in Wales for about five hundred years, the Romans invaded and eventually conquered the Celtic tribes. In time, many Celts decided to leave their own villages and follow a Roman way of life. As a result, many Celtic villages fell into ruins.

Given these problems, archaeologists have had to dig the ground in the places where they think the Celts lived to find clues about their houses and homes. This can be a hard and tiring job since they have to look carefully through the earth and rubble for bits of evidence. Historians, who study mostly written records, can also help. Although the Celts left no written records, the Romans, who later invaded Britain, wrote a lot about the Celts. The Roman accounts do not always tell us about the things we would have really liked to have known and they are often very one-sided!

•   Can you think of any other ways you could find out more about the Celts?

9

What archaeologists think a Celtic village looked like

On the basis of evidence it is possible to put together a picture showing what a Celtic village and house might have looked like. In some parts of Wales today, people have actually rebuilt Celtic villages from this evidence. You can see these **reconstructions** of Celtic villages in a number of places, including the Museum of Welsh Life, St Fagans near Cardiff, Castell Henllys in west Wales and Dan yr Ogof in the Swansea Valley.

A Celtic village

Archaeologists are fairly sure, through looking carefully at the patterns on the ground, and the earth and stones around the sites, and photographs taken from the air, that each village was surrounded by a wooden fence, built on top of a bank of stones, and covered with earth. This was called, in Welsh, 'bangorwaith'.

The word 'bangor' was often used to describe the site of a
Celtic village.

- Imagine you have come across what you believe is
  the site of a Celtic village. Explain how you would go
  about the task of trying to find out more about the
  site.

- Using a map of Wales, make a list of any places in
  Wales today called 'Bangor' or which have the word
  'bangor' in their name.

Archaeologists also found that the fence around the
village was usually made by knocking pieces of wood into
the ground, about five hundred centimetres apart, and then
weaving pieces of hazel stick between the upright wood to
make a wattle fence.

Bangorwaith
(wattle fence)

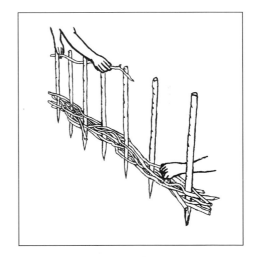

Inside this fence, the archaeologists found the remains of
round houses, arranged in the shape of a circle. Most of the
houses would have been about four to five metres in
diameter. They found that there were no divisions within
the houses to create smaller 'rooms'.

The walls in these houses were made in much the same way as the fence around the village, except that daub (wet mud) was placed on the wattle for protection against the wind and rain. In some houses, stones rather than wattle and daub were used. Inside the walls, thick poles were hammered into the ground. Long, but slightly thinner poles, were then fastened from the walls to the thicker poles inside the house to support the roof. The roof was covered with straw or rushes.

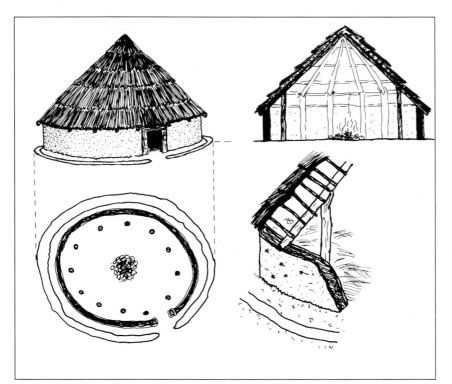

Plan of a Celtic house

Archaeologists also discovered ashes in the centre of the round houses where fires had once burnt. From other evidence, the archaeologists believe the houses had no chimnies but rather a small hole in the roof for the smoke to escape. There were no windows either, although animal skins were put over the entrance to keep out the cold. The earthen floor was usually covered with rushes or straw.

Celtic house with stone walls

THE CELTIC HOME

Inside a Celtic house

The second picture on page 13 shows an artist's reconstruction of the inside of a Celtic house based on what both archaeologists and historians have been able to find out. In the picture a man is tasting broth or soup boiling on the fire. Although this might suggest that men helped with the cooking, this was rarely the case. Most of the time, the men were busy farming, hunting and fishing and left almost all the work in the home to the women and younger children.

Let us look more closely at the some of these tasks in the home.

Making cloth

The Celts really enjoyed wearing brightly coloured cloths. These cloths were made by the women and children. First of all wool was gathered from the sheep and spun into a thread. This was done by tying a weight to the end of the wool and carefully twisting the wool, making sure that the thread did not become too thin and break.

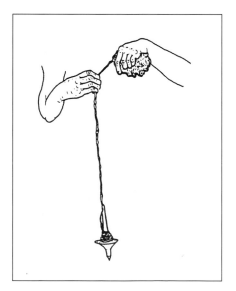

Spinning by hand

14

After spinning, the wool was dyed with the juice from crushed berries found on trees and bushes around the village. It was soaked in the dye for a long time. The wool was then woven on wooden looms. The thread was carefully passed in and out of the upright strands of wool and then knocked together using combs made of bone.

Bread making

The picture below is an artist's reconstruction of a woman grinding maize or oats on a quern or large stone.

Grinding oats

You might like to try grinding oats or wheat yourself using stones. This might give you some idea how long it would have taken to grind enough to make flour for all the family. Once the flour had been mixed with milk and a little butter it was slowly baked on the fire on a large flat stone.

Making broth

Broth or soup was made in a large cauldron hung on a cord tied to the roof. The broth was made from vegetables, such as peas and beans, and wild plants found in the countryside. Oats and barley were sometimes also added to the broth. Weeds too often found their way into the cauldron.

Farming and looking after the animals

Apart from work inside the home, there was always plenty of work to be done outside. The Celts planted a number of crops including peas and beans, although the main crops were oats and barley. They used to plough the fields with a wooden plough called an 'ard', pulled by oxen. The Celts cut their crops with iron sickles.

Using oxen to plough

The Celts also kept sheep, cows and horses. Men and older boys looked after the animals. At night, and throughout the winter, the cattle were brought inside the village fence and fed on hay, dried leaves and bark.

• Look at the list of statements below. Some of these statements depend on what archaeologists have found out, whilst others could not have been discovered by archaeologists alone. Put a tick by the statements which depend on what archaeologists could discover and a cross for those which depend on other types of evidence. Explain your decisions.

Statements:
1. A fence was built around the village.
2. The whole family lived together in the same house.
3. The roofs of Celtic houses were covered with straw or rushes.
4. A fireplace was built in the centre of the house.
5. Animal skins were put over the entrances of the houses.
6. Celtic men spent most of their time farming, hunting and fishing.
7. The Celts enjoyed wearing brightly coloured cloths.
8. Flour was made by grinding maize on a large stone or quern.
9. A cauldron was hung on a cord tied to the roof.
10. The Celts cut their crops using an iron sickle.

HOUSES IN THE MIDDLE AGES

Historical background

In 1066, following the battle of Hastings, William, Duke of Normandy, became king of England. In the years that followed, he took land away from the English landowners and gave it to the Normans who had fought for him. About twenty years later William and the Normans began to attack parts of Wales. Eventually, as they conquered parts of Wales they began to build, at first wooden, and later stone castles. The remains of many of the stone castles can still be seen in many parts of Wales. Although many of the Normans lived inside the castle walls, other Normans built their own houses.

Tower or first floor houses

In some areas of Wales where the Welsh and the Normans often fought each other the Normans built tower houses or first floor halls. These were usually built of stone and the people lived on the first floor. This could only be reached by a ladder. The ladder was pulled up at night. You can still see the remains of these houses scattered around certain parts of Wales. Most of the best examples are in south Pembrokeshire.

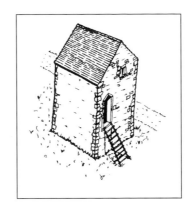

Medieval tower house

The houses and homes of the Welsh people: the Hendref and the Hafod

Many people in Wales, however, continued during the middle ages to live in houses very similar to the ones they had lived in before the Normans arrived. These were known as hall houses because they had only one large room or hall and only one floor. The hall had an opening in the roof at one end and the room was heated by an open fire with no chimney. The walls of the hall house, like the houses of the Celts, were made from wattle and daub and the roof was thatched with straw. The windows had no glass, and shutters were used to keep out the rain and control the draughts.

Inside a hall house

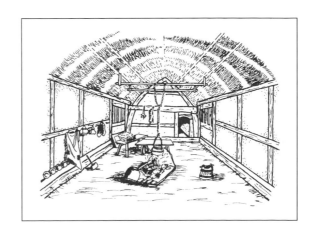

There is a description of a hall house in an old Welsh story called 'The Dream of Rhonabwy' in a collection of stories called the Mabinogion. In the story two travellers arrive at the house of a man called Heilyn Goch.

'And as they came towards the house, they could see a black old hall and smoke a-plenty from it. And when they came inside, they could see a floor full of holes and uneven. Where there was a bump upon it, it was with difficulty a man might stand thereon, so exceeding slippery was the floor with cows' urine and their dung. And when they came to the main floor of the house they could see a raised platform, and an old woman feeding a fire, and when cold came upon her she would throw a lapful of husks on to the fire. And the woman lit a fire of sticks for them and went to cook, and brought them their food, barley-bread and cheese and watered milk.'

These hall houses, called the 'hendref', would have been built in the more sheltered valleys and lowlands which gave protection to the people and their animals.

These people, however, would not have lived there throughout the year. Between the months of May and September they would have moved with their sheep and herds to smaller houses on the higher ground. These houses, known as the 'hafod', were often simple buildings made of stone or sometimes wood, with the roof covered with clumps of earth or reeds.

This movement of people from the hendref to the hafod for the summer months continued in Wales for many centuries after the middle ages. Here is how a writer called Thomas Pennant described a family living in Llanberis, Caernarfonshire in 1791:

'The hafod consists of a long low room, with a hole at one end of the roof to let out the smoke from the fire which is made beneath. Their furniture is very simple; stones are substituted for stools and beds are of hay along the sides. Towards winter the family moves back to their Hendref or old dwelling where they led, during that season, a vacant life.'

- Why do you think people moved from the hendref to the hafod in the summer months?

- What do you think would have been a) the advantages b) the disadvantages of this way of life?

- Some houses in Wales today are named 'hendref' or 'hafod'. Using a map of your local area, depending on where you live, you might be able to find houses with these names.

TUDOR HOUSES AND HOMES

Historical background

At the end of the fifteenth century, after Henry Tudor defeated Richard III at the battle of Bosworth Field in 1485, life for some Welsh people slowly began to change. The new king, Henry VII, was a Welshman and some Welsh people, who had helped him become king, went to London to serve Henry. Some also made fortunes whilst in London. Although some of these Welshmen decided to stay in London, others eventually returned to Wales. They were given important positions, such as sheriff and justice of the peace, and helped the king in the areas where they lived. In 1536 another important step was taken when a law was passed by the English parliament uniting Wales and England. In the years that followed, more and more Welsh people went to England and began to copy English ways. Some of these people, when they returned to Wales, built houses in a style similar to those they had seen in England. In time, these were copied by people who had never even been to England!

People built two new styles of houses in Wales in the Tudor period: wooden-framed houses and stone houses. Some half-timber, half-stone houses were also built. These new houses were often called **Tŷ Mawr** (Great House), or **Plas** (Place or Palace).

Timber houses

Maes Mawr, Caersws: a timber-framed Tudor house

Timber houses were usually built in separate sections ready for putting together. They were probably made in a carpenter's yard and then carried to where the house was to be built. Houses were put together, a piece at a time, with each part marked so that the builders would know where it fitted.

The first thing that had to be done was to cut down oak trees and shape them into planks to build the frame of the house. Cross-pieces of timber were fixed with wooden pegs to the upright timber.

Timber frame and wattle

The whole frame was then lifted into position and the gaps were filled with wattle. To finish the walls, the wattle panels were plastered with a thick layer of daub. The roof was usually covered with thatch of either reed or straw, although in some houses tiles were used.

Stone houses

In some other parts, and especially in north and west Wales, many houses were built of stone. Sometimes these were given the names **Tŷ Maen** (stone house), or **Tŷ Newydd** (new house). Most of the stones used to build these houses were brought from local quarries, although in some cases stones were used from older buildings. Some old castles built in the middle ages were pulled down to build these houses. Monasteries, most of which had been closed by Henry VIII, were also demolished to provide stone.

The best stone, often limestone, was used around the windows and doors. The stones were held together with a mortar made from lime.

TUDOR HOMES: MAKING LIFE MORE COMFORTABLE

During the Tudor period, a number of important new developments took place in the way houses were built. These helped to make the houses much more comfortable to live in.

Glass

Glass windows appeared in many houses for the first time. At the beginning of the Tudor period glass was still hardly used. But by the end of the century, as glass became cheaper, it was put into many of the larger new houses, although the windows themselves were usually still quite small. Glass windows, by keeping out the cold, rain and draughts, made houses much more comfortable.

Fireplace and kitchen

Another important development was the enclosed fireplace.
Before that time, an open fire had almost always been lit in
the middle of a room. Now, in the Tudor period, large
fireplaces and chimneys began to be built for the first time.
In some houses these were big enough to hold a bench so
that people could actually sit inside the fireplace. This type
of fireplace was called an 'inglenook'. In timber houses,
the fireplace too was often made of wood, although stones
were placed around the fire itself.

*Tudor
fireplace*

Fires were kept lit day and night. Fires helped to keep
the house warm and dry and were very important for
cooking. The smell of cooking and baking would probably
fill the whole house. In some of the larger houses boys
were used to turn the spit that held the roasting meat above
the fire. This was a very hot and uncomfortable job.

Wood was usually burnt on the fire. Many rich people
used wood rather than coal because they preferred the
smell. It was said that coal reminded them of hell and the
Devil!

Some homes had separate kitchens. Meals were prepared here for the family, and this is where the servants ate. Meat and bread were sometimes cooked or baked using a large covered pan and placing the pan in the fire surrounded by embers.

- Compare the kitchen in your own home with the kitchen described above. Make a list of the differences you notice in the way food was kept and how the food was cooked.

Food

The kinds of food that people ate depended on how rich or poor they were. Foreigners who visited this country mentioned that the rich ate a lot of food, especially meat.

Rich families often ate large meals. Although there were a large number of dishes on the menu, people did not eat everything. Here is what a sixteenth-century writer wrote:

'When they have taken what it pleaseth them, the rest is reserved, and afterwards sent down to their serving men and waiters, who feed thereon in moderation, and what they do not want is given to the poor which lie ready at their gates in great numbers to receive the same.'

The rich landowners would invite perhaps fifteen or twenty guests to a meal. Food was served in a particular order. The food was first placed on the 'top' table and then passed from table to table. The more important you were the sooner you were served.

'The first course served at the Master's table consisted of boiled meats, boiled beef, roast veal, rabbits and pigeon pie. The second course: roast lamb, rabbits, chickens, kid and moorcocks, baked chickens, moorcock pie, lamb pie, soused pig, tarts. Plenty of choice so far as meats were concerned, but no vegetables mentioned.'

The very rich people often used silver plates and drank from expensive crystal goblets. Less wealthy people would use pewter cups and plates. On most ordinary days of the week, rich people ate all kinds of meat together with bread, and drank ale . Diseases were caught because people did not eat enough fresh vegetables or drink much milk. Their teeth too usually went black at an early age.

Manners when eating were as important then as now. Here is a poem reminding people how to behave:

> 'Scratch not thy head with thy
> fingers when thou arte at thy meate;
> Pick not thy teeth with thy knife nor
> with thy fingers ende;
> Fyll not thy mouth too full, lest thou
> perhaps must speak;
> Nor blow not out thy crums when
> thou dost eate.
> Foule not the place with spitting
> where thou doest sit.'

The richer people ate bread made from wheat. Poorer people, however, had to eat what they could get. Bread made from rye or barley was their main food. When times were hard they made bread from beans, peas or acorns. They did this by boiling the ingredients two or three times. This was then dried and ground into flour to make bread.

Furniture and other possessions

We know a lot about the furniture and other things owned by landowners and farmers in the sixteenth and seventeenth centuries because they left lists or inventories of what they owned. The wealthier a person, the more items there were on the list. Here is an inventory of the things that belonged to a man named Alexander Bodvell who lived in Caernarfonshire in north Wales in the seventeenth century:

IN THE CELLAR	4 HOGSHEADS OF BEER
IN THE KITCHEN	1 BRASS CAULDRON 4 SMALL PANS WOODEN DISHES 1 BELLOWS
IN THE DINING ROOM	2 CHAIRS 10 STOOLS
IN THE UPPER LOFT	12 HOBBETS OF MALT 4 HOBBETS OF OATS

IN THE KITCHEN LOFT	2 FEATHER BEDS
	3 BOLSTERS
	3 PILLOWS
	3 BLANKETS
	3 BEDSPREADS
IN THE SMALL LOFT	2 FEATHER BEDS
	BEDCLOTHES
	PEWTER DISHES
IN THE HALL	2 CHAIRS
	2 STOOLS
	1 CUPBOARD
IN THE PARLOUR	1 FEATHER BED
	2 CHAIRS
	2 STOOLS
MR LLOYD'S CHAMBER	1 CHEST
	2 STOOLS
	2 CUSHIONS
	1 CARPET

Many of the words in the list might seem strange to you. Here is the meaning of some of these unusual words.

* A **hogshead** contained 36 gallons or 162 litres.
* **Pewter** was made from a mixture of lead and tin. It was made into dishes, pots and mugs. Poorer people would use wooden dishes called platters. (Lead is considered dangerous today and would not be allowed to be used

for dishes).

* A **bolster** was a long under-pillow on a bed. It was the width of the bed and smaller pillows were placed on top. People of this period did not sleep lying full length on the bed. The pillows helped them to sleep sitting up.

* **Hobbets** were measures of grain.

- If you were to make a list or inventory of items in your house, in what ways would it be a) similar to and b) different from Alexander Bodvells' list?

HOUSES AND HOMES IN THE WELSH COUNTRYSIDE: THE EIGHTEENTH AND NINETEENTH CENTURIES

THE HOUSES OF THE RICH

Historical background

In the eighteenth and nineteenth centuries, some landowners who owned acres of barren mountains suddenly became very rich when mining and quarrying for minerals such as copper, lead, slate, iron and coal started on their land. Although some of these landowners decided to employ men to mine or quarry themselves, others leased the rights to other people for huge sums of money.

As the landowners grew wealthier, they began to build larger and grander houses than any that had been seen in Wales before. These houses or mansions were built away from any farm buildings and were surrounded by large parks and were approached along gravel roads.

Plas Glynllifon, near Caernarfon, Gwynedd

These new houses, such as Glynllifon shown above, were extremely large with as many as thirty or more rooms. The front of the houses were also carefully planned. The front door was often surrounded with pillars and decorations based on ancient Greek and Roman designs.

Each side of the door there were often oblong windows, all of the same size, which opened with the help of cords and weights.

Pillars found in large houses

Sash window

- Look for examples of pillars and sash windows in houses or other buildings around where you live.

Directly behind the front door there would often be a grand staircase. Every room in the house could be approached from the central hallway. Each room was private and each had a special purpose — the drawing room, the dining room, the billiard room, the library and sometimes even the ballroom.

Life in the houses of the rich

Many of the owners of these houses enjoyed entertaining their friends, and particularly enjoyed riding and shooting parties on their huge estates. They appointed stewards to run their estates and to collect the rent from their workers.

These houses also had a large number of servants to clean, cook, wash clothes and look after the fires. The servants were expected to do everything quietly and carefully. In many houses, the servants used stairs at the back of the house so that they did not mix with the family. Often they slept in small rooms in the attic. At the back of the house were the kitchens, bakery, laundry, storerooms and sometimes stables.

This is a description of life in St Fagans Castle, written by one of the servants named Mary Ann Dodd in 1870:

'We worked from 6 am until we finished. I helped to make the beds and then every day I had to grind the coffee and make the water biscuits. The coffee came from Scotland, a hundredweight (50 kilos) at a time.

I had 37 pieces of copper to clean each day. There were about forty-seven people in service in all and we were a very happy staff. I earned around two shillings (10 pence) a day.'

- Why do you think so many servants were needed to run these large houses? Describe the life of
  a) a landowner and b) a servant in a large house during this period.

By the end of the nineteenth century, there were over a million and a half girls and women working as servants in Wales and England. After the First World War (1914-18), however, as servants' wages and the price of food and goods began to rise, the owners found they could not afford to keep so many servants. It also became difficult to keep large houses in good repair, as very high taxes or death duties had to be paid when an owner died. As a result, many homes were sold to become hospitals, hotels or schools while others were left empty and fell into ruin.

THE HOUSES OF THE POOR: Tŷ unnos

Historical background

Although some very large houses were built in Wales, many poor people struggled to survive in very badly built houses. These 'houses', if in fact they could be described as such, were often not that different from the kind of houses in which people had been living centuries before.

In the late eighteenth century there was a great increase in the number of people living in the Welsh countryside. This caused many problems as there was not enough work for everybody. Some people, many of whom had no work at all, were forced to built simple shelters, usually on waste and barren land. This land was not fenced and people thought they could live there without permission. In fact, this common land was usually the property of a landowner, but because it was poor land, the landowners did not, at first, force people to leave. The people who settled on this land, known as squatters, believed that if they were able to start building a house at dusk one evening and have smoke coming out of the chimney by dawn the next day, they had a right to live in the house. This is why the houses were called in Welsh 'tai unnos', or one-night houses.

Building a 'tŷ unnos'

You may have wondered how it was possible to build a house in such a short time. Fortunately, some of the people who wrote about what Wales was like at this time asked the squatters to describe how it was done. This is what one person wrote:

> 'The person who wanted to build the house and his friends arrived at the place where they wanted to build the house at nightfall and started to cut square

clods of turf. When a quantity of the turf had been cut, some of the men commenced building up the walls with the clods, and when it was sufficiently high the previously prepared roof was quickly put on and thatched with straw and rushes, so that the roof should be completed and smoke coming through the chimney before the sun rose. All this being done the builder could say "My house is my castle". The amount of land around the house was then decided by his throwing an axe from the door in various directions, the hedge being planted along that line.'

Houses like this were certainly built in Wales up to a hundred and fifty years ago. In 1847, a government inspector described one of these houses in Rhayader, Radnorshire, as a 'house without a window or opening except a doorway, not watertight and only one room'. Yet, nothing now remains of these houses. In fact, we cannot even be sure where they had actually been built. Often the houses were only lived in for a year and then left to fall down. As you can imagine, living in such a house must have been a miserable experience, with water leaking in most of the time. No wonder people did not stay in them for very long!

- In what ways were the 'tai unnos' a) similar to, and b) different from the houses of the Celts?

- Why do you think people have been unable to find evidence of any 'tai unnos', even though many were built just one hundred and fifty years ago?

THE FARM WORKER'S COTTAGE

The people who did manage to find some work often rented
cottages from the landowners or farmers, usually for a year
at a time. Here is what was written about a cottage in
Pembrokeshire in 1814:

> 'A mud walling about five foot (1½ metres) high, a
> low roofing of straw and with a wattle and daub
> chimney, kept together with a rope bandage, and
> slanting to the side. The roof was thatched with reeds
> or straw.'

Cottages like this could still be found in some parts of
Wales one hundred years ago although by that time most of
the newer cottages were built with stones.

Cottage shown in Land Report of 1894

Cottages like this one, whilst certainly very much better than the 'tai unnos' and those made from wattle and daub, were often still poorly built. The walls of these cottages were made of stones, often a metre thick, with mud and rubble mixed together to fill in the gaps. Here is what a government inspector wrote about a cottage he visited in Talyllyn in Caernarfonshire in 1847:

'The house is wretched. The cottages are formed of a few loose stones, piled together without mortar or whitewash. The floors are of earth; the roofs are wattled and many of these hovels have no windows.'

- In what ways might these cottages be considered to be better than 'tai unnos'? In what ways could these cottages have been improved? Can you think of any possible reasons why such improvements were, in many cases, not made?

Inside a worker's cottage

Conditions inside many cottages were often very poor. Most had only one room. This room was sometimes divided into two parts by placing a bed or other piece of furniture across the middle of the room. Since there was no tap water, the people had to collect water from a stream or river nearby. There were often no drains either. Here is how a government inspector described such cottages in 1893:

'The cottages are built by unskilled men to no definite

plan. A tapering hole in the roof serves as a chimney, but more often than not the smoke escapes by the door or oozes through the gaps in the walls. Many cottages have peat fires.

A great proportion of the cottages have no toilets attached, and where they are, they are seldom used. The people seem to have an objection to using them'.

Living in such a house was often very hard and many people, particularly the children, frequently suffered from illness and disease. Most such families also kept a pig, which often shared the cottage with the people. Here is what a traveller named William Bingley wrote about when he visited one such cottage in 1803:

' Around one table sat a family eating bread and milk, the usual food around here. From a bucket placed for it in a corner a large fat sow ate its food while I ate bread and butter in the other'

But gradually, in the second half of the nineteenth century, as many workers moved from the countryside to the towns to find work, farmers found it was not quite so easy to get farm workers. As a result, they had to make sure that their workers' cottages were improved. Some of the older cottages were simply pulled down and rebuilt using the old stones. Despite this, you can still see in many parts of Wales piles of stones where a cottage once stood.

THE FARMER'S HOUSE AND HOME

Throughout Wales today, there are many different types of farms and farmhouses. Some farms are large, employ many workers and cover a large area, whilst others are quite small and are farmed by just one farmer and his family. The shape and size of the farmhouse and other buildings also differ from farm to farm. We will now look at one type of farmhouse once found in many parts of Wales — the Welsh Long-House.

Long-House

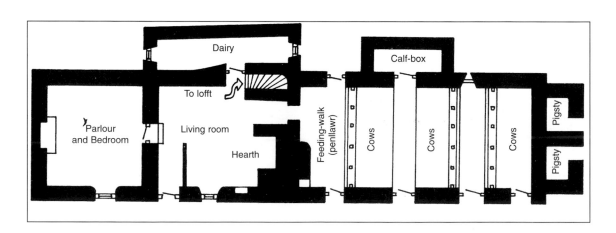

Plan of a Long-House

The unusual thing about these houses was that the farmer, his family and the animals lived under the same roof. At one end of the building was the farmhouse and at the other end the cattle lived throughout the winter. In between the two parts of the house was a narrow passage called the 'penllawr'. The floor of the cattle shed was usually built lower than the rest of the house. The fireplace in the farmhouse was always built on the wall next to the 'penllawr'. The farmhouse itself was often split up into a number of smaller areas using furniture.

- What do you think were a) the advantages and b) the disadvantages of designing a house in this way?

Life for the farmer and his family, as for the other people who worked on the farm, was often hard. Many farmers and their families were little better off than the workers they employed to help them on their farms. The only difference between them was that while a farmer could be sure of some work, the farm workers could not.

HOUSES IN NINETEENTH-CENTURY TOWNS

Historical background

During the nineteenth century more and more people moved from the countryside to the towns to look for work.

Some even decided to leave Wales altogether and went to live in countries like America and Australia. Many others went to live in England. But more found jobs in the ironworks and coalmines of south and north-east Wales and the slate quarries of north Wales.

As a result new towns and villages were built and expanded quickly. But there were problems. Most of these people certainly could not afford to buy their own house. In some cases, the men left their families in the country while they found work and a place to live. Often, at first, they lived in lodgings with many other men. Eventually, however, once they had found a job and earned some money, they were able to rent their own house. Soon, their wives and children would join them. Let us look more closely at what such houses were like.

Terraced houses in Mountain Ash

Terraced houses

The ironmasters, coal mine and quarry owners usually built
houses for their workers near to where the people worked.
Because so many people needed houses, the owners found
it was much cheaper to build the houses in terraces or rows.

Slum houses in Cardiff: Ivor Street, about the year 1900

- What were the advantages and disadvantages of
  building houses in this way?

Most early terraced houses were badly built and were
described as 'slums'. Many had no drains or tap water. The
people often suffered from bad chests and breathing
problems caused by living in these poor houses. But the

disease people feared most was cholera. This was caused by people drinking dirty and polluted water. When cholera broke out in Cardiff in 1849, an inspector, Thomas Rammell, was asked to find out more about what conditions in the slum houses were really like. Here are some of the things he heard or saw:

> 'Mary-Ann Street and David Street are densely populated; there is only one pump there. It is used for drinking; it is not the best of water, I have seen worms in it; the people clamber over the wall for this water, it is like a struggle for life and death. In Waterloo buildings, near the Hayes, there are eleven houses with two privies (toilets); one toilet was full-up to the seat-board and full of filth.'

Many of these houses were overcrowded too. Here is what Thomas Rammell saw in one such house:

> 'I inspected several houses in Stanley Street, amongst others a lodging house kept by Michael Harrington. I counted the persons living in the house; there were 54 persons, men, women and children; they live, eat and sleep all in one room. The smell arising from the overcrowded room is most overpowering.'

Not all houses, however, were as bad as these and many were certainly much better built than those in country areas. Roofs were made of slate, they had more than one room, the walls were usually dry and the windows could be opened.

As time went by, the government passed laws to try to get the really bad slums pulled down. They also passed stricter rules about how houses should be built. The quality of materials improved. New roads and railways made it possible for every house to have slate, good stone, bricks, glass and wood, even if these had to be carried by rail or road over long distances from other parts of the country

The two drawings on page 46 show how the inside of some houses also changed during this period. The first is a living room from a house in the 1840s. It shows examples of the plain furniture that families brought with them when they moved from the countryside to the towns; the second drawing is very different and shows a typical living room in a terraced house in the 1890s.

- Make a list of the differences between the two drawings.

Even at the end of the nineteenth century and in the early years of this century, many houses still had no running water. Many houses still had no indoor toilets, although outdoor toilets, usually at the bottom the garden, were sometimes connected to drains.

1840s

1890s

Life in the home

Housework was hard. In the days before electric washing machines, washing would start very early on a Monday morning and continue all day. The washing would be done outside in a wooden tub, and the water heated in a big iron boiler. Plenty of hot water was always needed.

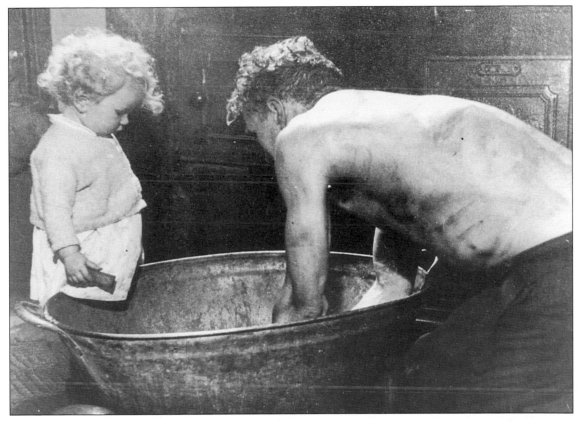

Coal miner washing in front of the fire at the end of his shift

The coalminers and slate quarrymen, in particular, got very dirty whilst at work and they would have a bath in a tub in front of the fire after work each day.

The floors of the terraced workers' houses were usually made of paving stones. Women would scrub and whiten them and take pride in keeping them clean. The outside doorstep was cleaned in this way too. The fireplace, where all the cooking was done, was regularly polished with blacklead, and all the brass was kept shining. While the women looked after the inside of the house, the men often spent hours after work looking after their gardens, growing vegetables for the family. Many men also had allotments where they grew extra food.

Food

Here is a list of food and other items which an iron worker and his family from Merthyr Tydfil bought in a month in 1839:

Flour, butter, sugar, tea, cheese, bacon or ham, fresh meat, potatoes, currants, raisins, blue, starch, pepper, mustard, soap, clothes, shoes, tobacco, beer, candles.

- Compare this list with the items your family would buy each month. What would candles be used for?

- This family bought 'blue' and 'starch'. Try to find out what they were used for.

From around 1860 onward, as wages rose, people found they could buy more with the money they earned. This allowed people to buy better food and more food. Higher wages even allowed them to buy a few luxuries. But life was still very hard for many families, many of whom continued to live in very poor houses without enough food or clothing.

CONCLUSION

We have now looked at a number of different types of houses, and examined the lives of the people who lived in them. Over the centuries, the homes and houses of the Welsh people changed a great deal, and are still changing today. Some of these changes have happened quickly, whilst others were spread over many centuries.

- Can you find examples of any of the types of houses described in this book near where you live? What other types of houses were you able to discover?

- You might also like to make a list of the ways these homes, built perhaps many years ago, have been changed as the owners have replaced older parts of their houses, or added to them.

The inside of most homes has also changed greatly. Today there are generally many more luxuries, including television sets, washing machines, fridges and central heating. The way we heat our homes has changed too: fewer homes burn coal on open fires and many more homes use other forms of heating. Certainly people who lived even a hundred years ago could hardly have imagined the changes that have taken place. Have you ever thought what houses and homes might be like in another hundred years?

- Make a table or chart to describe the different types of houses you have read about in this book. There is a pattern for you to follow on the next page.

Type of House (down the page)

Celtic Houses
Norman First Floor Houses
Medieval Welsh Houses
Tudor Houses
The Houses of the Rich (eighteenth and nineteenth centuries)
The Tŷ Unnos
Squatter Houses
Welsh Long Farmhouses
Terraced Houses

Headings to describe houses (across the top of the page)

*   Building the house
    Headings: Walls Roof
*   Inside the house
    Headings: Floor Doors Windows Fireplace
*   Life of the people
    Headings: Food Housework Work around the house

Put a cross if the heading does not apply to a particular type of house.